FINANCIAL MANAGEMENT

BULLET GUIDE

Philip Ramsden

Hodder Education, 338 Euston Road, London NW...
Hodder Education is an Hachette UK company
First published in UK 2011 by Hodder Education
This edition published 2011
Copyright © 2011 Philip Ramsden
The moral rights of the author have been asserted
Database right Hodder Education (makers)

Artworks (internal and cover): Peter Lubach
Cover concept design: Two Associates

All rights reserved. No part of this publication ma... form or by any means, electronic, mechanical, ph... writing of Hodder Education, or as expressly perm... rights organization. Enquiries concerning reprodu... Department, Hodder Education, at the address a...

You must not circulate this book in any other bin...

British Library Cataloguing in Publication Data: a...

10 9 8 7 6 5 4 3 2 1

The publisher has used its best endeavours to ensure that any website addresses referred to in this book are correct and active at the time of going to press. However, the publisher and the author have no responsibility for the websites and can make no guarantee that a site will remain live or that the content will remain relevant, decent or appropriate.

The publisher has made every effort to mark as such all words which it believes to be trademarks. The publisher should also like to make it clear that the presence of a word in the book, whether marked or unmarked, in no way affects its legal status as a trademark.

Every reasonable effort has been made by the publisher to trace the copyright holders of material in this book. Any errors or omissions should be notified in writing to the publisher, who will endeavour to rectify the situation for any reprints and future editions.

Hachette UK's policy is to use papers that are natural, renewable and recyclable products and made from wood grown in sustainable forests. The logging and manufacturing processes are expected to conform to the environmental regulations of the country of origin.

www.hoddereducation.co.uk

Typeset by Stephen Rowling/Springworks

Printed in Spain

Durham County Council
Libraries, Learning and Culture

C0 1 70 50582 3X

Askews & Holts	
658.15	

In memory of my dad, Brian, whose idea it was that I should do accounting at university, when I thought about doing maths. If I hadn't listened, I doubt I would have written any of my books. On the other hand, I might have ended up at NASA…

About the author

Philip Ramsden is a Fellow of the Chartered Institute of Management Accountants, although as a colleague once told him, 'you're not like a normal accountant'. He suspects this is because he was one of those rare ones that explained things to people, instead of trying to confuse them with numbers and terminology. On the other hand, it may have been something to do with his passion for chocolate…

He is the author of several books on finance and has even somehow managed to get chocolate into this one. He likes writing, skiing and chocolate, possibly not in that order. He absolutely loves his wife, fell walking and rum truffles. Best to say in that order.

Contents

	Introduction	vii
1	The profit and loss account	1
2	The balance sheet	13
3	Cash flow control	25
4	Fixed assets and depreciation	37
5	More about cash	49
6	Ratio analysis	61
7	Budgets	73
8	Basic bookkeeping	85
9	Trading entities	97
10	Project evaluation	109

Introduction

The accounts, the numbers, the figures: those simple words can turn professionals, experts in their field, into mild-mannered onlookers who lower their heads in meetings. Meanwhile, the financial wizards weave their magic, summoning balance sheets, depreciation, overheads and other terms that might as well be written in ancient runes.

You don't necessarily want to be an accountant – but you'd like to understand what's going on. This book grants you a gentle introduction to the world of **business finance**, throwing light on the shadow talk of accountants, while displaying a healthy interest in chocolate.

By the end, you will be conversant with common **financial terminology**, able to listen with understanding during the finance sections of those meetings, and even able to offer the odd comment. Armed with the knowledge from this book, and possibly a small bar of chocolate, you will impress – more so than those who didn't read this book.

1 The profit and loss account

P&L: the main financial report

The **profit and loss account** is the headline grabber: 'Banks make record profits/losses!!' depending on which decade it was…

The P&L account, as we will call it from now on, is probably best viewed as the main financial report. Its main purpose is to state the profit, and show how it (or a loss) was made. It also monitors and measures revenue and costs.

> **The profit and loss account shows how the profit or loss was made. Duh!**

The P&L account reveals the figures for trading over a certain period, usually a year, although the management of a company will also get a monthly version.

So how does a company go about making a profit or loss? At the simplest level, such as in statutory accounts (available from Companies House in the UK for a small fee for all limited companies), the details behind the P&L account are:

1. sales
2. cost of sales
3. overheads (including expenses)
4. interest received/paid
5. taxation.

This chapter tackles these one at a time…

P&L: key terms

Sales

Sales (or revenue) is the amount the company has received, or is due to get paid, for its goods or services. This doesn't include VAT, because that is owed to the Inland Revenue, not for the company to keep.

Cost of sales

Cost of sales is the cost of buying in goods or materials, plus the costs of manufacturing to get those materials into a saleable state. It can be more complicated than that, but, since this is the absolute basic version of finance, we'll stick with that.

> **CASE STUDY: Cost of sales**
>
> For a high street retailer selling chocolate, the cost of sales is the cost of buying it from the manufacturer. For the manufacturer, it is the cocoa, sugar and other ingredients, and the cost of getting them into the packaged form.

Sales less cost of sales gives a figure the accountants like to call **gross profit,** although, just to confuse people who might be getting to grips with accounting, it can also be called the **margin.**

> **'Money is better than poverty, if only for financial reasons.'**
> Woody Allen

Overheads

Overheads generally fall into two categories:

* administration
* distribution.

Overheads cover any kind of non-manufacturing expenses, such as those relating to Finance, IT, Research and Development, Despatch and other non-production departments.

And what kinds of **expenses** might we find in overheads?

P&L: more key terms

Expenses

There's a whole host of types of expenses, and this list therefore is by no means exhaustive:

- salaries
- national insurance contributions
- pension costs
- equipment hire
- advertising
- journal subscriptions
- patent licences
- conference fees
- postage, printing
- consultancy fees
- rent and rates
- legal fees
- cleaning
- flowers (those plants in reception don't come free)
- car hire
- photocopying
- depreciation (see chapter 4)

and, of course, stationery.

● Expenses, expenses...

Bullet Guide: Financial Management

Profit = sales less costs

Expenses must fit in one category or another to come off the gross profit. So sales minus cost of sales is gross profit, and by reducing it further with expenses, we get…

Profit before interest and tax

Let's call it **PBIT**, and deal with the I and the T:

Interest paid or received

This is the same as might be applied to an individual. Money in the bank earns interest; overdrafts and loans incur it. Cash-rich companies, such as superstores, can generate millions in interest.

Taxation

People pay income tax; businesses pay corporation tax. It is roughly 30 per cent of profit above a certain level, but with a complex set of rules and calculations that keeps taxation specialists in the higher bracket of income tax.

A typical P&L account

P&L Account for Concocted Company Ltd
to the year ending 31 December 2012

	31.12.2012 £000	31.12.2011 £000
Revenue	15,400	14,750
Cost of sales	7,365	6,902
Gross profit	8,035	7,848
Administration expenses	2,861	2,677
Distribution expenses	2,744	2,902
Depreciation	305	280
Operating profit	2,125	1,989
Interest payable	45	35
Tax	512	433
Profit attributable to shareholders	1,568	1,521

You get two for the price of one: the previous year's figures are usually there for comparison.

Bullet Guide: Financial Management

Note that:

* **Sales** have here been called **'Revenue'**, but it's the same thing. And it's the same with PBIT/operating profit.
* These are in **thousands of £s** (the '£000' means that), so revenue is just over £15 million, profit over £1.5 million.
* You don't get much detail on the expenses, though managers of the company will, in their 'accounts pack'.
* **Depreciation** (we'll look at this later) gets its own line sometimes; it's that special.
* The last line, what might be called **net profit,** is what gets added to the **shareholders' profit reserve** in the **balance sheet,** less any **dividends** they take.

● 'And here is the net profit!'

Visualizing the P&L account

Let's make it look a bit more interesting:

Concocted Company Ltd: profitability to year ending 31 Dec 2012

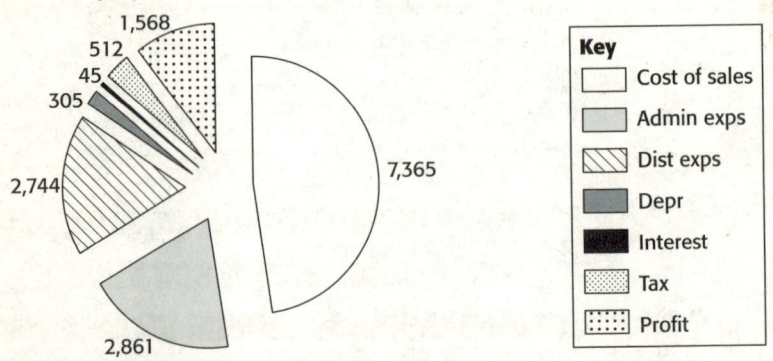

Key
Cost of sales
Admin exps
Dist exps
Depr
Interest
Tax
Profit

1,568
512
45
305
2,744
7,365
2,861

- Pie chart presenting the P&L account graphicallly

This is (almost) the same information, just presented differently. The pie chart doesn't include revenue.

Bullet Guide: Financial Management

The profit

So after all that, we've arrived at 'the profit'. For all that some people appear to be against profit making, the alternative is that a business makes a **loss** – and any business that does so consistently is likely to close down, with subsequent loss of jobs.

High profits, however, might suggest there is scope for cutting sales prices – the result of which might have more social benefits than business ones. Here is a quote that many business managers ought to bear in mind:

> **'Annual income twenty pounds, annual expenditure nineteen nineteen six, result happiness. Annual income twenty pounds, annual expenditure twenty pounds ought and six, result misery.'**
>
> Charles Dickens

2 The balance sheet

What is a balance sheet?

The **balance sheet** is a key financial statement, purporting to represent the 'value' of an organization on a given day. This chapter explains the constituent elements of a balance sheet.

The balance sheet is the company's financial position *on a given day*

The three main categories of a balance sheet are:

1 **assets** – what the company has
2 **liabilities** – what the company owes
3 **equity** – what is due to the shareholders.

Larger businesses may have balance sheets with bigger numbers in, but the formats are the same no matter what size the business is.

The balance sheet, as its name suggests, must balance, so that:

assets = liabilities + equity

'Balance is beautiful.'
Miyoko Ohno

Each of these categories contains elements that must be managed.

Fixed assets

The definition of a fixed asset varies, but it is generally a **tangible** item (or an intangible one associated with a tangible item) costing more than £1,000 that will last for more than one year. For example, a forklift truck is considered a fixed asset (even though it moves). We'll look again at fixed assets in chapter 4.

Are these fixed assets?
- ✔ forklift truck
- ✔ new motor for chocolate grinding machine
- ✔ architect's fees for a chocolate factory
- ✘ maintenance costs for chocolate-melting oven
- ✘ new tyres for the distribution fleet
- ✘ a tonne of cocoa beans

Bullet Guide: Financial Management

Categories of fixed assets
1. Land and buildings
2. Plant and machinery
3. Office equipment
4. Vehicles

● 'You're just stock. I'd be a fixed asset!'

'No one has a greater asset for his business than a man's pride in his work.'
Mary Parker Follett

Net current assets

Also called **working capital**, net current assets are traditionally defined as:

current assets − current liabilities

Current assets
* Stocks
* Debtors
* Cash

Current liabilities
* Trade creditors
* Other creditors
* Overdraft

'The greatest asset a head of state can have is the ability to get a good night's sleep.'

Harold Wilson

Bullet Guide: Financial Management

Current assets

Stocks

Stocks are items that are manufactured or bought in:

* **materials** to be processed
* **work** in progress
* **finished goods** ready for sale.

It's all the stuff in the warehouse or on the shop floor, or in the shop.

Debtors

This is the amount owed by customers, and can also include prepayments – things the company has paid in advance for (such as insurance).

Cash

This is not literally what money is the bank; it's the amount in the **cashbook.** It works on the same principle as your cheque-book stub (if you're one of those rare people who still use a cheque book, or the even rarer type who fills the stub in), taking into account cheques yet to hit the bank and unlodged receipts.

Current liabilities

Creditors

* **Trade creditors** – what is owed to suppliers.
* **Other creditors** – amounts owing to VAT, Pay As You Earn (PAYE, which is income tax collected from employees), and perhaps employees if they are paid in arrears.
* **Accruals** – an amount for goods and services received which haven't been invoiced yet.

> Amounts owing to creditors also include **accruals,** which refer to accounts on a balance sheet that represent liabilities.

Overdraft

Companies have them, the same as the rest of us. Only bigger.

'Creditors have better memories than debtors.'
Benjamin Franklin

Working capital

This is the same as net current assets (although another definition excludes cash). It is a measure of a company's short-term financial health.

- **Positive working capital** is held to be a good thing – in theory, the company could sell all its stock, get all the money in from customers, and be able to afford to pay off all its creditors.
- **Negative working capital** means that the company is unable to meet its short-term liabilities with its current assets. This is not necessarily a bad thing, however: it may be the norm for that industry. Or maybe not…

Net assets (also known as capital employed) = fixed assets + net current assets

Two more things…

Long-term liabilities

The principal difference between these and the liabilities in net current assets is that these are *not due for more than one year*. Good examples are:

* **long-term loans**
* the amount outstanding on **leased items** (rather than bought fixed assets).

Liabilities do not include the apparent inability of some managers to run their company!

Equity

In theory, equity is the amount due from the company to its owners, the **shareholders.** This comprises **capital investments** made by the shareholders, plus any reserves.

The major reserve is the **retained profits** figure, which is the accumulated profit of the company after dividend payments to the shareholders. The increase in the reserve for this year is this year's profit, which comes straight from the profit and loss account.

Bullet Guide: Financial Management

Submitting the balance sheet

Limited companies have *nine months after their financial year end* (the date the balance sheet was prepared) to submit it to Companies House (in the UK) or its equivalent, for public availability.

So how much is a company worth? Here are some recent approximate values of some well-known companies:

BP	$250,000 million
Lloyds TSB	£50,000 million
Sainsbury's	£10,000 million
Tottenham Hotspur plc	£300 million
Thorntons	£60 million

Note BP's figure in dollars – to make sure you're comparing apples and apples!

3 Cash flow control

The importance of cash flow

Cash is absolutely vital to a company, but cash is not the same as profit. Even a profitable company can go under owing to lack of cash.

To take an extreme example – running a woodland – you plant a few saplings or seeds, and 20 years later, after nurturing your stock, you'll have a fine forest of mighty trees ready to be turned into snooker tables, matches and quality furniture. The saplings cost you mere pennies; the trees will sell for hundreds of pounds.

Cash is not the same as profit!

Quids in – except that for 20 years, it's been all spend, spend, spend:

* fence repairs
* pest control
* equipment hire for trimming
* chocolate while you tend your trees

and whatever else goes on in woodland management. It will be profitable after the 20 years, but what are you going to live on in the meantime? Acorns?

● In another 20 years…

The cash flow cycle

A business can survive for some time when making losses, but if it is suffering from more cash flowing out than in, it may struggle to keep going.

For this reason an organization's **cash flow cycle** has to be *managed*. The flow of cash is really simple:

* **Your debtors** are the customers who pay for the goods and services you sell to them.

* **Your creditors** are the people you pay for the goods and services you receive from them.

But what if your **customers – the debtors** – want 'trade terms of paying in 60 days'?

'No problem,' you say.

But, say I again, what if your **suppliers – your creditors** – want paying in *30 days*?

Bullet Guide: Financial Management

Where does the money come from to pay the suppliers if the customers haven't settled up yet? And that's not taking into account paying wages and factory costs to make the finished goods…

The local bank might be friendly and understanding, and allow a temporary overdraft, but at an interest rate that might make you want think of another strategy.

The strategy is to manage the cash flow.

● 'One day I'll be quids in…'

'Happiness is a positive cash flow.'
Fred Adler

Managing the cash flow

A good way to manage cash flow in your company is to consider the three elements of **working capital:**

1 stock
2 debtors
3 creditors.

Buying stock means owing the supplier, who becomes a creditor. Debtors owe the company money, with due dates for payment. Creditors will want paying when their invoices are due. Planning the timing of these leads to a cash flow plan. And if you have a plan, you can see where it went wrong!

● Manage that cash flow!

Bullet Guide: Financial Management

Stock

* Buy as little stock as possible, because it will have to be paid for.
* However, make sure there is enough to meet production/sales requirements – **lost sales mean lost profit/cash**.

Debtors

* A sale isn't a sale until it's paid for (something all salespeople should commit to memory!).
* Shorter credit terms mean you should get paid sooner.

Creditors

* Longer credit terms mean you can keep your money in the bank for longer.
* If money is tight, **prioritize payments** – wages, statutory bodies (VAT and national insurance). Key suppliers tend to be high on the list.

Basic rules of cash flow control

1. Try to sell on **shorter credit terms** than you have to pay on – that way money comes in before it has to go out.
2. Don't buy **too much stock** – it might need paying for before you've sold it.
3. Indeed, if *any* purchase can be reduced, deferred or avoided, it will mean less cash going out.
4. If a customer's payment is **overdue** – ask for it!

Don't buy too much stock

● Pay me now!

Who is responsible for cash flow?

The sales force

* They not only make the sales, but also set the credit terms.

The buyers

* These can be those who order the stock for production, a manager hiring a fork-lift truck, a secretary ordering stationery, R&D, subscribing to journals…indeed, anybody who has the authority to buy.

Accounts people

* They are usually those in the credit control section who chase up payments from customers, plus the financial accountant doing the weekly payment run.

So that's pretty much **everyone** in a company.

Profit is good (see chapter 1), but remember: **'Cash is king!'**

Anon.

'It's not a sale till you get paid.'

CASE STUDY: Demand payment or give credit?

'We heard a rumour of a medium-sized customer of ours being in financial difficulties, although they had nothing outstanding with us. Then a fair-sized order, for over £20,000, came in from them.

'Our finance guy (me!) was wary and suggested payment up front, but our sales director reckoned they'd be OK. Besides, it was a big sale for us, it would have made the month's figures look better, and if we didn't supply on credit, someone else would. The two of us begged to differ (actually we were at loggerheads!).'

Which way would you have jumped?

Bullet Guide: Financial Management

CASE STUDY: What happened next?

'A Board decision was made – to sell, on a reduced 14 (instead of the normal 30) days' credit.

'One week later, the customer went bust. Cue one embarrassed sales director, one slightly smug financial dude, and one quick-thinking managing director who sent our trucks round to grab our stock back.'

If this were a fable, the moral would have been: 'It's not a sale till you get paid.'

4 Fixed assets and depreciation

What is depreciation?

This is the one that seems to scare people – **depreciation.** You'll be OK, promise.

Depreciation is simply the *cost* of something spread over several years, not the buying of it over that period. The main thing with buying fixed assets is that you don't deduct the cost of them from the P&L account in expenses when they happen.

Let's repeat the **fixed assets** idea, and add a bit more detail.

Depreciation is the *cost* of something spread over several years

A fixed asset is usually a **tangible** item – something you can see or touch – that costs more than £1,000 and will be in use for more than a year.

Intangible items associated with a tangible one can be included, so for example:

* a new mould for a giant chocolate aardvark is a tangible fixed asset
* you can add on the designer's fees for it even though it's an intangible item – you can't touch them, but you won't get a mould without them.

These expensive items would put a very large dent in the profits of a company in the year they bought them, so, rather reasonably, the accountants spread that expense over the years the items are in use. And that is what they call **depreciation.**

CASE STUDY: Spreading the expense

A distribution company runs its lorries for three years before replacing them; they cost £60,000 each to buy. It replaces ten of them, spending £600,000, which would be a big dent in the annual profits in the year they bought them – but years two and three would be 'free' (apart from running expenses), since they're not replacing these new lorries until year four.

The accountants therefore spread that expense over the three years the lorries are in use: £600,000 over three years, that's…£200,000. A depreciation charge is made to the **P&L account** of £200k in each of the three years.

'A child of five could understand this. Send someone to fetch a child of five.'
Groucho Marx

Let's clarify a really important point from the case study opposite: *how* the company pays for the lorries **does not affect the depreciation**.

1. They may fork out the whole £600,000 in one go.
2. They may pay in instalments.
3. They may take out a loan for them.

That's the **cash** side of things, and it has no bearing on the depreciation, other than that the totals must be the same. All clear now, I hope.

● 'Totally clear!'

Categories of fixed assets

Because different things wear out over different time periods, accountants make things easier for themselves and put fixed assets into various **categories,** usually:

1 land and buildings
2 plant and machinery
3 office equipment
4 vehicles

and then depreciate items in each category at the same rate.

**Typical depreciation rates of fixed assets
(p.a. = per annum = each year)**

Land and buildings	land (0% – it never wears out)
	buildings (25 years = 4% p.a.)
Plant and machinery	5 years = 20% p.a.
Office equipment	5 years = 20% p.a.
Vehicles	3 years = 33.3% p.a.

Bullet Guide: Financial Management

Gross and net book value (GBV and NBV)

The initial cost of the item, the lorries or building or whatever, is called the **gross book value** (GBV), and appears, if you recall, in the balance sheet. It is an asset of the company.

Then there is the **annual depreciation charge,** calculated as a percentage of the initial cost, charged as an expense to the P&L account each year.

* The **total depreciation** charged against each asset since it was bought is the **'accumulated depreciation'**.
* This can be deducted from the GBV, giving the **net book value** (NBV), which is a line you will see in the balance sheet.

GBV − accumulated depreciation = NBV

CASE STUDY: The cocoa bean grinder

The cocoa bean grinding machine has been running for two years, and so it has had two years' worth of depreciation. It's had £5,000 charged to the P&L account for each of those two years, so that's £10,000 altogether. So it will have a book value, on the balance sheet, of:

Gross book value (its original cost)	£25,000
Accumulated depreciation	£10,000
Net book value	£15,000

One possibility

What if the machine actually lasts for only three years? By then it has an **accumulated depreciation charge** of 3 x £5,000 = £15,000, so a net book value of £25,000 − £15,000 = £10,000. According to the accounts, that's what it's worth.

Bullet Guide: Financial Management

But the Production Department are complaining it's breaking down too often, and needs replacing now, not in another two years. Let's not let the accounts get in the way of making good business decisions – it's got to go.

The solution

We can sell it for scrap for £2,000. First we 'write off' the £10,000 value it has on the balance sheet, then add back the money we've got for it:

Net book value	Proceeds from sale	Loss on disposal
£10,000	£2,000	£8,000

That final figure appears in the P&L Account, usually as a separate line, because it's not related to the normal trading operations.

> **'If you count all your assets, you always show a profit.'**
> Robert Quillen

Another possibility

On the other hand, what if it's a well-made grinder and lasts for seven years?

* After five years, it will have a **nil net book value:** the accumulated depreciation charged equals the original cost; it has been 'fully written off'.
* According to the books, it's **worthless**, but Production loves it – it works, it's reliable – can they keep it?
* Of course they can. In fact, they get 'free' use of it, as there's no more depreciation charged.

In the real world, there's many a 20+-year-old lathe turning away without a problem, which according to the Accounts Department has no value, but still does a sterling job.

> **'When I was young I used to think that money was the most important thing in life. Now that I am old, I know it is.'**
>
> Oscar Wilde

To summarize...

Depreciation is the cost of a fixed asset charged to the P&L account over a period of years.

It is **not:**

* the company putting aside that amount of cash each year to get ready to pay for a new one
* the company paying the supplier that amount for it each year.

Depreciation has **nothing** to do with the cash flow involved with buying the asset.

There you go. You have it now, depreciation sussed.

● Happy dance...

5 More about cash

Concepts about cash

There are two major concepts to think about here. We've already looked at one of them briefly, but it's so important that it's worth getting into a bit more detail. They are:

* **profit v cash** (revisited)
* **cash v accruals**.

It's no coincidence that cash features heavily; as I keep stressing, it's essential.

> **It's no coincidence that cash features heavily – it's essential**

You might think the example of running a woodland we looked at chapter 4 a little extreme, and you would be right. So let's think about another business starting up:

* You and I are going to go into **partnership**, and we're going to **retail** ultra-delicious chocolates made by monks in a Swiss valley.
* We plan to do this **via a website**, because if we had a shop full of the stuff, our quality control costs (i.e. me sampling them) would be exorbitant.

In this chapter we'll explore the themes of profit v cash (revisited) and cash v accruals through our joint **business venture**.

Profit v cash

Setting-up costs

1 We'll need a **website** designing and hosting.
2 We have to let potential customers know who we are and what we have, so there's **marketing** to be done.

I think we should plan no more than £5,000 to get our product known to a favoured few. I'm hoping £1,000 will cover the website stuff, because we can both do a bit of that ourselves.

If you can't do that or the marketing, I hope you're good at negotiating buying the choccies; otherwise this is becoming a one-sided partnership!

Agreeing terms

The suppliers don't know us, and we have no trading history; they don't know if we're going to be in business long enough to pay them in the **usual 30 days' terms** they give everyone else. So we'll have to **pay up front**. It's not a problem – we've got £10,000 starting money between us.

Bullet Guide: Financial Management

Let's get to the chocolates. Our monks are nice people, but their chocolate is truly scrumptious and accordingly expensive. We could price ourselves out of business if we try to charge too much, so we go for a **markup of just 10 per cent.**

A big hit!

It's going to take two weeks before the marketing has an effect, and because this isn't yet a real business, I'm going to ignore delivery costs, and the administrative expenses that inevitably crop up in real life.

And I'll say our product is a big hit. On the following page you'll see what the **sales** are like, along with the **costs**. In fact, it's our **P&L account** for the first two months.

● 'It's a hit!'

Our P&L account

P&L

Week	1	2	3	4	5	6	7	8	Total
Sales					10,000	20,000	20,000	30,000	80,000
Cost of sales					9,091	18,182	18,182	27,273	72,728
Gross profit					909	1,818	1,818	2,727	7,272
Marketing	5,000								5,000
Website	1,000								1,000
Profit	(6,000)*	0	0	0	909	1,818	1,818	2,727	1,272

* Figures in brackets indicate a loss.

Bullet Guide: Financial Management

We can't charge people until delivery is confirmed, which turns out to be **a week after the sales order.** So let's look at the **cash flow** for the same period.

> *We're really getting those chocolates out the door, aren't we?*

> *Yes, but you're our biggest customer!*

'Success is having to worry about every damn thing in the world, except money.'
Johnny Cash

Our cash flow

Cash flow

Week	1	2	3	4	5	6	7	8	Total
Sales						10,000	20,000	20,000	50,000
Cost of sales					(9,091)*	(18,182)	(18,182)	(27,273)	(72,728)
Marketing	(5,000)								(5,000)
Website	(1,000)								(1,000)
Net cash flow	(6,000)	0	0	0	(9,091)	(8,182)	1,818	(7,273)	(28,728)
Cumulative	(6,000)	(6,000)	(6,000)	(6,000)	(15,091)	(23,273)	(21,455)	(28,727)	

* Figures in brackets indicate cash flowing out.

Yikes! We put only £10k in ourselves (which I haven't shown above), and, after two months, we need £28+k – we have to get another £18k+ from somewhere!

'Yikes! need more cash!'

- We're already **in profit**, and, even if we kept at the same level of business as week 8, making another £2,700 a week, we'd generate over £100,000 in profit in a year!
- If things stay the same, cash flow in week 9 is good – £30k in, £27,273 out, net receipts of £2,727. At that rate, we'll **break even in cash** in 11 more weeks (11 x £2,727 will bring us just over £28k).

Profits are good, but cash takes some time to catch up

Thinking about it, I'd rather be a customer, and just enjoy the chocolate...

Cash v accruals

This one's a bit simpler, although unfortunately it doesn't involve chocolate. Go on, then, it will…

The Swiss monks use a secret ingredient in their fine products, made from the crushed berries from a bush that grows in the neighbouring valley. Once a week, the farmers bring up the harvested berries.

However, these people are good farmers, not accountants, and sometimes take a month or two to get round to invoicing the monastery.

'What the world really needs is more love and less paperwork.'

Pearl Bailey

> Brother Paulinus, who does the accounts for the chocolate business, is not daft enough to think the berries are free when the invoice doesn't turn up that month. So he uses an accounting technique to put the cost of them into the accounts for that month *as if an invoice had been received* – this is an **accrual**. And that's all there is to it.

So when your accountant says she's going **to accrue** for something, all she means is the cost or expense will be reflected *in the accounts in the period in which that activity occurs.* The paperwork can catch up later.

The invoice can be paid months later, and that will affect the cash – but the reduction in profit is already accounted for.

I can't believe that those monks want to pay us for this stuff!

They don't! You always forget to invoice them!

6 Ratio analysis

What are financial ratios?

Be honest: if I say this next bit will involve some maths, are you going to say, 'Agh! I can't do maths!'? You've done all right so far, so stick with me. It's baby maths…

Ratios are simply *one number divided by another.* The trick is to use the right numbers. A ratio by itself is not enough, however: *the important point is having some sort of comparison.*

Ratios are simply *one number divided by another*

Bullet Guide: Financial Management

Having a value of 7, for example, tells you nothing, but knowing that another company scores 4 on the same ratio, or that your own last year was 6, suggests that things might be going well for you. Some **favoured ratios** are:

- ROCE
- current ratio
- quick ratio
- gearing
- interest cover
- dividend yield
- EPS
- P/E.

These are the commonly quoted ones, and sound impressive when used with someone who doesn't know what they are… 'I see Thorntons' ROCE is up 0.2%' is a phrase you can drop in at your local golf club, skateboard park or Swiss monastery and receive admiring glances… possibly.

ROCE

ROCE is short for **return on capital employed,** and is pronounced 'Ro-si'. The idea behind this is that if you have some assets, say a house you let out, and it generated some income and expenses to leave you with a profit, what sort of return are you getting?

If it's 0.5 per cent, wouldn't you have been better putting your money into a bank and getting, oh, say, 0.7 per cent? (Not really, because you hope the house value will go up over the years, but that's a different topic.)

The point is that companies' assets are used to run the business, and generate the profit. So the formula for ROCE is:

Profit before interest and tax/capital employed

'Watch the costs and the profits will take care of themselves.'

Andrew Carnegie

Bullet Guide: Financial Management

The figures come straight from the P&L account and balance sheet, where **capital employed** is the **total net assets**. Companies use variations to this formula, but this is a common one.

Remember!
The key thing is not so much what the value is, but *how it compares* to last year's, a major competitor's, the industry average, etc. A ROCE of 6.5 has more meaning if you know last year's was 4.1, the market leader's is 8.8 and the industry average is 7.1.

● 'I'm not taking part in this race until I know your ROCE, Mr Rabbit...'

Current ratio and quick ratio

Current ratio and quick ratio are similar to each other.

Current ratio

* This is calculated by dividing the **current assets by the current liabilities,** and poses the question:
  » If this company got all its debtors to pay up, and sold all its stock at face value, and added in its cash, could it pay off all its creditors?
* A score of 1 or more says yes.

Quick ratio

* This is the same but excludes stock, possibly on the grounds that a firm trying to offload it desperately may not get much for it.
* This ratio will always give a lower value than the current ratio.

Top tip
Use these ratios to **compare and contrast** with last year's ratio and those of other companies.

Gearing

Gearing measures the extent to which a company is funded by loans. It's a good example of **investor-type ratios**, for those pondering a dabble on the stock market, and in these days of stocks and shares ISAs, unit trusts and invested pension funds, that's pretty much all of us. It sounds complicated, but isn't.

Most companies borrow money to finance their activities. It costs a lot to build factories and even call centres. The more a company borrows, the harder it is to pay back. Gearing is:

loans / (loans + equity capital)

This tells who is putting the money into the company's activities – lenders or shareholders – so who is taking the risk.

If the answer's too high – say over 80 per cent (i.e. a lot is coming from lenders) – new lenders might be wary. But again, see how any result compares to the industry average: 80 per cent might be the way that industry operates.

The interest cover ratio

Similarly, lenders are going to want to know that the interest a company owes them is going to be paid. To work it out, they don't just look at the profit figure and see that it's enough; they use the **interest cover ratio**:

profit before interest and tax / interest charged

* This tells them *how many times the profit could have paid the interest.*
* You'd have thought once would have been enough, but this gives an idea of the company's profitability relative to the loans to finance the business.
* This also shows how easily the company can pay interest on its outstanding loans.

● 'With your interest cover ratio you should have been able to pay me by now!'

Dividend yield

Shareholders use another source for some of their ratios: stock market prices. Companies pay a dividend to their shareholders, usually twice a year, and shareholders can work out their return:

Note!
This ratio ignores the longer-term potential of the share price rising to generate an additional gain when the shares are sold, but it's a reasonable way of comparing different companies' dividend policies.

dividend yield = dividend per share / share price

If I stick some cash in an ISA, I might get interest of 3 per cent. If, instead, I buy some shares, what return will get back? **Dividend yield** will tell me this.

'How do you make a small fortune on the stock market? Start with a large one.'

Investor adage

Earnings per share

You can decide which company to invest in by looking at **earnings per share (EPS),** calculated as:

(profit after tax − preference dividends) / number of ordinary shares issued

* A company's published accounts will give you the figures.
* EPS means *how much profit each share in the company generates.* That gives you an idea of the potential for **dividend payment**.
* More profit means more dividend for you and me, so more chocolate.

● 'I'm only interested in the earnings per share because I need to pay for my chocolate addiction...'

Bullet Guide: Financial Management

The P/E ratio

Finally, the often-quoted **price-earnings (P/E) ratio** (simply referred to as the PE ratio) works out a company's current share price compared to its earnings per share. It's calculated as follows:

market price per share / earnings per share

* You will hear people say that this is a multiple of how many times the earnings can be bought with each share. If it's too high, the shares are deemed expensive.
* This is a particularly good one for *comparing companies in the same industry.*

What's a good value to decide if shares should be bought? If I knew that, I'd be writing this from a chalet neighbouring a certain Swiss monastery…

The PE ratio: good for comparing companies in the same industry

7 Budgets

What is a budget?

The Chancellor of the Exchequer has one, individuals have them, companies certainly have them. For all of them, a budget is a **plan of income and expenses.**

If a company does not have a plan of what it intends to do, it has no idea if it is achieving what it wants to, or even what it should be doing. Setting a corporate budget is usually an annual activity.

Budgets should, in theory, be based on the company's **five-year strategic plan,** and evaluated against its goals.

The problem is that budgets take a lot of work:

* If companies have a financial year end of 31 December, many will start on the following year's budget in July.
* Sales and Marketing will be asked what figures – volumes and prices – they expect next year, when still only halfway through the current year.
* It's a bit of a guess, but can be an educated one when Accounts give them helpful figures such as sales this year (by customer and/or product).

Budgets start off as a plan, but can become targets

Planning a budget

It's the same principle for costs and expenses. Once the sales volumes are agreed, production costs can be calculated, with a budget for:

* number of **hours** of production needed
* number of **staff** needed
* amount of **material** needed at what price

…and so on. Departmental managers will look at this year's spend, estimate overheads by the end of the year, and work out a budget for the following year.

● Oh no, budget time again!

All this leads to Accounts doing a lot of number crunching, and the figures bouncing back and forth, until senior managers like the look of what they see, and the budget is eventually agreed. This might be done from either the 'bottom up' or the 'top down'.

Bottom up approach	Top down approach
The staff or management who cause those sales and costs get to set their own figures.	The figures are imposed by senior management: 'We command revenues of £25.6 million next year.'

In practice, it's usually something in the middle, although senior management will always have the final say.

'To fail to plan is to plan to fail.'

Attributed to Winston Churchill, Benjamin Franklin and possibly my careers teacher, Mr Archer

Meeting – or not meeting – the budget

Why is it so difficult to get people to agree what the numbers should be? Because when that budget year starts for real, and actual results come in month by month, there will be a difference (referred to as a **variance**).

And if it's a negative one – say actual sales are 10 per cent under budget – questions will be asked. What was a plan has now become a **method of control**.

● The monthly sales review meeting gets under way…

Reasons for not meeting the budget

The **sales manager** may make several **defences**:

1 Her original figures for the budget were fairly close to the actual, but she was obliged to change them because top management didn't think they were high enough (especially if they have higher management to impress).
2 The figures were done months ago – how was she supposed to know a major customer was going to go bust, or that strong competition didn't allow for projected price increases?

It's the same with **production**:

1 Currency rates might have forced imported materials to cost more.
2 Unforeseen staffing problems might have affected fulfilment.
3 There might be unexpected problems with equipment, causing production downtime.

If the figures are under budget, questions will be asked

Phasing and other problems

Even with **overheads,** there could be phasing problems.

> **CASE STUDY: Budgeting in action**
>
> Human Resources budgeted £25,000 for recruitment costs, just over £2,000 a month. But a need arose to get a couple of new engineers into R&D pronto, so they had to spend £6,000 in the first month. **Overspent already** – but since there would probably not be any more such expenditure for several months, the budget would 'catch up' with the year-to-date expenditure.

There is really no way round this – **sometimes the budget is just wrong**. Senior management rarely accept this view, and demand that their managers improve their efforts to restore sales, cut expenses and get the organization back on track to meet the budgeted profit.

Budgets as targets

One reason why a budget may be wrong is that it goes from being a **plan**, then a **controlling comparison**, to being a **target**, and used to measure performance:

- Managers might be paid bonuses on meeting or, usually, exceeding budget.
- **Sales and profit** are usually the key driving figures behind such rewards.

'Budget: a mathematical confirmation of your suspicions.'
A. A. Latimer

Some uncharitable minds might suggest why the salespeople in a certain company weren't keen on sales being budgeted at £25.6 million: they may have genuinely believed £22 million a more sensible figure, but it would also improve their chances of a bonus.

Unexpected items

There will also be a budget for balance sheet items, including **fixed asset expenditure.** There will be a list of 'big ticket' items that the company is thinking of spending money on in the budget year. That's good, that's planning.

What can then happen is that during that year, some need will arise for an **unexpected purchase** – maybe an upgrade to the IT system because orders have gone through the roof – and the IT manager is met with the reply, 'It's not in the budget. Plan for it next year.'

It might really need doing, but some people seem to think 'It's not in the budget' means it can't be done. Frankly, that's nonsense.

Business decisions need to be made on a **business and economic rationale,** so the proper response is

'Never confuse the budget with reality.'

I said that.

CASE STUDY: 'It's not in the budget.'

The seven-year-old cocoa bean grinder was still clanking away (see chapter 4) and doing a good job, despite having no accounting value. Even if money for a new one is in the budget, it is **not compulsory** to buy one.

On the other hand, the chances are that if Production don't get a new one now, next year's budget won't have one included either, so if 'Old Grinder' crunches its last cocoa bean then, a request for a replacement will be met with 'It's not in the budget'.

Buy the new grinder, or there will be no more chocolate!

8 Basic bookkeeping

Credits and debits

I'm not here to turn you into a bookkeeper, or even an accountant. I just want you to understand what finance is about. So apologies, but we're going to have to get down and dirty with a little insight into the detail.

Every transaction you make will lead to (at least) two entries in your accounts, a debit and a credit. Debits and credits form the basis of the **double-entry bookkeeping** system.

What used to happen (up to the introduction of computers, and about the 400 years previously) is that when a transaction occurred, it was written down, in a book, twice – one entry for the **credit,** another for the **debit** – hence the term double-entry bookkeeping.

In this system, for every debit transaction there must be a corresponding credit transaction, and vice versa.

Here's an example, of selling something to someone for £100, **in cash:**

* Credit sales   100
* Debit cash   100

If you think of credit as plus, and debit as minus, each transaction adds up to **zero**.

Think of credits and debits as just pluses and minuses

Why is cash a debit?

This is a brief digression, because I don't want to confuse you. 'Why is cash a debit? A cash balance is a credit on my bank statement.'

There are two reasons:

1 It needs to be a debit to keep the double-entry system **balanced**.
2 This is how the bank treats it: when you deposit money, the bank owes it to you – you are their **creditor**, so they credit your account, and debit their cash figure. Your bank statement is reflecting the **bank's accounting position** rather than yours.

> **'A bank is a place where they lend you an umbrella in fair weather and ask for it back when it begins to rain.'**
>
> Robert Frost

Let's do the sale again, except the customer is going to owe the money instead, and pay it later:

First, the sale:	Later, the payment:	What happened in the debtor's account:
Credit sales 100	Credit debtors 100	Debit 100 (when the sale was made, and the customer owed the amount)
Debit debtors 100	Debit cash 100	Credit 100 (when the customer paid up)

In summary:

✻ +100 − 100 = 0 – the customer doesn't owe anything any more.

And that's how simple double-entry bookkeeping is.

When bookkeeping gets complicated

It only starts to get complicated when:

* **several accounts** get debited and credited by a single transaction
  » For example, an invoice from a supplier for a desktop PC, stationery and chocolate will debit fixed assets (for the PC), the stationery account and the staff confectionery expense account, as well as the VAT account, and credit creditors.
* there are **thousands of transactions** to process
  » Even then, individually they are all done in the way described, and, besides, we now have shiny computers to do all the hard work.

> Even when bookkeeping is more complicated, the principle of each entry netting out to zero remains.

The ledgers

The ledgers are the **financial records** – the books of double-entry bookkeeping, if you will – of an organization. There are three main types:

1 Debtors' (or sales) ledger

This is also known as **Accounts Receivable**.

Detailed by customer, it lists the *invoices* sent to them (and any *credit notes*), less any *payments made*, the balance being how much the customer still owes. Add them all up, and you get the debtors' figure on the balance sheet.

2 Creditors' (or purchase) ledger

This is also known as **Accounts Payable**.

This is the same as above, but for suppliers – they send their *invoices*, we knock off *payments made*, and what's left is what is still owed. This shows as 'trade creditors' on the balance sheet.

3 General ledger

This is the main ledger, the financial bucket into which all transactions are poured. This is where all those debits and credits go.

The chart of accounts

The general ledger includes a **chart of accounts** that lists all the codes to which transactions can be made. They might look something like this:

00152503400	Sundry chocolates
00152503500	Sundry marshmallows
00152503600	Sundry chocolate biscuits

…depending how it has been set up, and what accounting software is used. There will be hundreds, possibly thousands, of such codes, if the company is big enough!

Using a good structure for the chart of accounts lends itself to good reporting. From the example given opposite:

* The **first three digits,** 001, might represent a division or company.
* The **next four** could be a department or cost centre (this is an area that has costs associated with it; see below), so the Accounts Department might be '5250' and Human Resources '5260'.
* Finally, the **last four** indicate the type of expense, so '3400' is chocolate.

This way, the computer can add up all the amounts in those codes with a '5250' in the middle to get the total costs for Accounts, or '5260' for HR. Totalling all amounts for codes ending '3400' will show much is being spent on chocolate.

● 'What's the code for chocolate buttons?'

What's a cost centre?

A cost centre is usually a division or a department that costs the organization money. The costs it incurs are allocated to it for reporting or control purposes.

If you think of a department like Production, it will contain areas for goods inwards, warehousing, assembly, inspection, etc. These will be cost centres, because there is expense (debits) in carrying out these activities.

Cost centres cost the organization money

There are numerous accounting books loaded with examples of debits and credits to help trainee accountants pass their exams (particularly the Financial Accounting one), but they are all based on the above **basic principles**.

● 'Debits and credits, debits and credits...'

Bullet Guide: Financial Management

Note!
The previous example, using Accounts as a cost centre, might be confusing terminology. (After all, the financial reports are also called 'the accounts', and they are produced by the Accounts Department.) It's a **cost centre** because debits and credits need putting in the right places, and the people in Accounts don't do it for free – they need paying salaries, and chocolate biscuits don't go amiss either…

It does get more complicated, but you've only had a few pages to unravel one of accounting's great secrets, so I think you've done well.

'If you want an accounting of your worth, count your friends.'
Merry Browne

9 Trading entities

Types of trading entity

In business, it can be important to know whether you're dealing with **one person** or **a company.** Throughout this book, I've generally used the term 'company', but in practice there are four different types of organization that are legally recognized:

1 sole trader
2 partnership
3 private limited company
4 public limited company (plc).

Are you dealing with one person or a company?

'You can judge a man by the company he keeps.'
Proverb

Factors that might influence the choice of business type include:

- the scale of the business
- the complexity of the business
- the type of business activity
- the importance of limited liability
- custom within the industry
- personal preference.

When a business starts employing people, it might be wise to look at **incorporation.** This is the noun for the formation of a legal corporation.

● 'Are you one person or a company?'

The sole trader

The most basic type of organization is the sole trader. A sole trader is that enterprising individual who starts up his or her own business.

* A sole trader is self-employed and may trade in his or her own name or register a business name.
* Sole traders can call their business whatever they like (within reason, and preferably if no one else uses that name), and this is their **trading name**.
* Any deals they do are done by the **individual**: that is to say, for any debts they incur, or any borrowings, the creditor is entitled to chase the individual for payment.
* The sole trader pays **income tax** on the profits of the venture.

'The art is not in making money, but in keeping it.'

Proverb

The partnership

A **partnership** is where two or more self-employed people work together as partners.

* They can decide **their own rules** about who does what and how the profit is shared, and who puts how much in to get it going.
* Once it is up and running, any action committed by one partner **commits all the others** – so a loan taken out becomes the responsibility of all.
* Profit, as with a sole trader, is subject to **income tax.**

● *'Our* debts, *our* profits...'

If it all goes wrong and you can't repay your loans, the bank will chase up all the partners, and if necessary, get them to sell their personal assets to pay the debts of the business. The creditors can have your house, your car, your chocolate fountain…

The limited company

But step forward, the **limited company**.

* By formally registering a company with **Companies House,** a partnership can become shareholders in a company.
* It is not difficult to do, but there are rules about company names and how many directors are needed.
* Unlike a sole trader or partnership, a limited company is not the same as the individuals who own or manage it.

The big advantage of a limited company is that, legally, it is viewed as a person in its own right. Debts are the responsibility of the company, not the shareholders (technically, their liability is limited to their share amount, which might be as little as £1, hence the phrase **limited** company).

A limited company is legally a person in its own right

So what's the downside? There are two major elements here:

1 You'll have to fill in several forms for Companies House at the financial year end, including **a copy of the accounts,** which usually have to be audited, so potential lenders can assess the risk.

2 Company profits are subject to **corporate tax;** and anyone who gets paid a salary by the company (which would include the shareholders, if they are also employees of the company) also pays **income tax** on their earnings.

Double whammy!

> **Top tip**
> Google Companies House and go to their website; it's extremely helpful. You do not need to pay someone £100+ to set up your company for you; it will do you good to get involved in the detail of what's required and do it yourself.

Public limited companies

Higher up the scale are **plcs** – **public limited companies** – and these include the ones you hear about on TV and in the press.

* They have **shares** anyone can buy, traded on the **Stock Exchange,** and the rules for their reports are much more stringent.
* The basic principles of **limited liability** and both **corporate** and **income tax** still apply.
* Like limited companies, plcs have to make their accounts **publicly available,** something a sole trader or partnership doesn't have to do.

> **Top tip**
> Most plcs will have their accounts on their websites, so you could go and find some and practise your understanding of P&L accounts and balance sheets, and even do some ratio analysis. Finish this book first, though!

Bullet Guide: Financial Management

Public disclosure

The **public disclosure** of a plc's accounts does mean that potential lenders, suppliers, investors, customers, even employees – and, crucially, competitors – can get some useful information about limited companies and plcs.

It's the price they pay for limited liability. That bloke selling Swiss chocolate on a market stall in Dundee doesn't need to tell anyone but the taxman about the numbers – not even his wife – but the plc must.

Top tip
Find out more about companies all over the world through this link: http://www.companieshouse.gov.uk/links/introduction.shtml

● 'My lips are sealed...'

What's in a name?

All trading entities, from sole traders to plcs, have restrictions on their trading name:

* Names shouldn't be too similar to an existing one if people might get the two confused.
* Sole traders and partnerships can't just stick 'limited' at the end of their name; that is strictly for properly registered companies.

How can you tell a registered company?
1. A **company registration number** should appear on their documentation.
2. With either the name or the number, you can check, in the UK, the **Companies House website**. From there, you can get the latest accounts, a list of directors, and other information, for a small fee.

Bullet Guide: Financial Management

Corporate structures

Normally, it is people – shareholders – who own a company. But a company can set up other companies, owning 100 per cent of the shares in it (or even jointly with other companies), creating a **group of companies**. This is not uncommon, and it:

- allows companies with diverse business interests to keep things separate
- allows these **subsidiary companies** to own other companies, creating a complex web of corporate ownership
- allows companies to spread overseas.

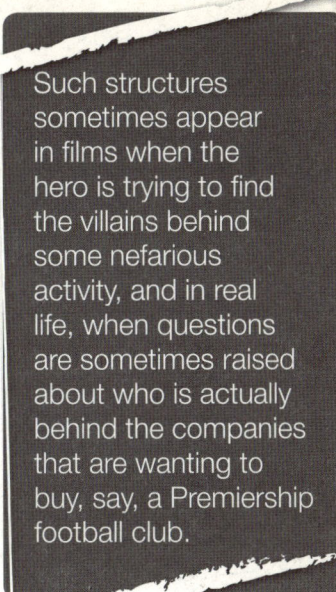

> Such structures sometimes appear in films when the hero is trying to find the villains behind some nefarious activity, and in real life, when questions are sometimes raised about who is actually behind the companies that are wanting to buy, say, a Premiership football club.

10 Project evaluation

Is the project worth doing?

You've handled plus and minus, and some division in ratios, so we're going to finish with some slightly harder maths as we look at how companies decide whether to spend money on **projects.**

Would you rather have half a kilo of monk-made Swiss chocolates now or tomorrow? Now, obviously; I can always get some more tomorrow. We'd always rather have something now than later, unless there'll be much more of it then.

We'd always rather have something now than later

Bullet Guide: Financial Management

But would you rather have:

* half a kilo **now**?
* 750 g **tomorrow**?
* a whole kilo of it **next week**?

It's the same for companies, only they think about money rather than chocolate. If there's a new product line being offered that's going to cost £400k to set up, but generate £950k in cash over the next five years, should they do it? Or just put the £400k in the bank?

● 'Ooh, tricky...'

'For years, I've kept a list of dream projects.'
Michael Bolton

The company cash flow

Let's imagine a rival chocolate company to our own. They've decided it's time for something new and exciting to boost their sales and profile. It's a big new project: a new line of chocolate, Belgium-style.

They need to know what the **cash flows** are. Fortunately they do:

Year 0	(400,000)	Year 3	250,000
Year 1	200,000	Year 4	200,000
Year 2	200,000	Year 5	100,000

These are the cash flows, not necessarily the **profit** (remember the difference!). The figure in brackets is what they have to spend to get the project going – new plant and machinery, marketing, additional salespeople, lots of things…

* From year 1 onwards, **net cash flow** is positive: there will be some expenses with marketing, distributing and selling the product, but income from sales.
* However, they are going to have to wait a year for it – that's not going to happen in practice because there will be receipts and expenses every day – but this is how these things work.
* Sales decline after year 3 (perhaps they think our monk chocolate will reduce their market).
* They think net income will be negligible after year 5, so it isn't included. Fair enough; this is best guessing anyway.

> So the total net income is £950k.

> But it's going to cost £400k to set up.

> Is it a goer?

Payback method

One way to evaluate a project is to ask this question:

When do they get their money back?

They spend £400k at the start; and by getting £200k back in each of years 1 and 2, they've recovered that outlay by the end of year 2. So the **payback period** is two years.

Most companies will usually want the payback period to be no more three years. Why?

Suppose the same total, £950k, was phased so that payback didn't happen until year 4, with all the excess income therefore coming in year 5.

What if the forecast was wrong?
What if it turns out to be a four-year product?

Bullet Guide: Financial Management

Net present value

Companies basically want their money back, and into a **positive cash position**, as soon as possible. But accountants are more sophisticated than that, and able to complicate things.

Remember how we said we'd rather have half a kilo of chocolate today than tomorrow? I said *I* would anyway…

That's because chocolate – and money – has a diminishing value over time.

* I'd need more to compensate me for waiting, and money also gets devalued by inflation.
* Getting £100k in Year 5 is not the same as getting it in Year 1.

So we reduce the value of future cash flows. The company selects some arbitrary figure, perhaps close to the cost of its borrowing money, but 10 per cent is easier to work with. So we **discount future cash flows** by that amount, multiplying the original cash flow in each year by the **discount rate**.

Doing the maths

To take the example of our rival chocolate company:

	Cash flow	Discount rate	
Year 0	(-400,000)	1.0000	(-400,000)
Year 1	200,000	0.9091	181,818
Year 2	200,000	0.8264	165,289
Year 3	250,000	0.7513	187,829
Year 4	200,000	0.6830	136,603
Year 5	100,000	0.6209	62,092
		Net present value	333,631

Multiply the original cash flow in each year by the discount rate

Bullet Guide: Financial Management

The discount rate column

Where does that discount rate column come from?

The **discount rate** reduces the value each year by 10 per cent, in this example.

* So year 1 cash flow is reduced by $1/(1+0.1) = 1/1.1 = 0.9091$
* In year 2, $1/(1+0.1)^2 = 1/1.21 = 0.8264$, etc.

Just to impress you, the formula is:

Net present value = $\Sigma\ 1/(1+i)^n$

where *i* is the discount rate, *n* is the year number, and Σ means add them all up.

● '*You* do the maths!'

Is the project a starter?

To find out, we would have to take the following into account:

1 That £100k in year 5 is reduced to being the equivalent of just over £60k today.
2 The project therefore has a total **net present value** (NPV) of just over £330k.
3 This means that if a competitor offered them £350k today *not* to start the project, they might as well take it.
4 Or if an alternative project had a higher NPV, that might be preferable.

Assuming all the figures come out right…

> 'Money talks; the secret is to hold it long enough to hear what it says.'
>
> W. G. Plunkett

Bullet Guide: Financial Management

That's it. You made it to the end; well done.

- 'Time for some celebratory chocolate...'